Contents

KU-418-274

Who was Victoria?

▲ Victoria's father, the Duke of Kent.

On 22 June 1897, crowds of excited people stood on the streets of London. They watched as bands, soldiers and carriages passed by.

In one carriage an old lady sat dressed in black clothes. She was Queen Victoria, and this was her Diamond Jubilee. She had been queen for sixty years. Victoria was the most famous person in Britain.

▼ Queen Victoria's Diamond Jubilee.

Our
Kings and Queens

VICTORIA

BUCKS COUNTY LIBRARY

20118

JB-VIC

SEP 2 6 2006

30 JAN 2008

MAR 2 0 2008

BUCKINGHAMSHIRE
COUNTY COUNCIL

This book has been
withdrawn from the
County Library stock
Price

Please return/renew this item by the last
date shown. Books may also be renewed
by phone and the Internet.

**Buckinghamshire Libraries
and Heritage**

www.buckscc.gov.uk/libraries

L.27

...tephen

...nal text by
...ood

WAYLAND

Our Kings and Queens

Titles in the series

HENRY VIII
VICTORIA

Editor: Jason Hook
Original design: Jean Wheeler
Cover design: Tessa Barwick
Differentiated design: Raynor Design
Text consultant: Norah Granger, University of Brighton

This edition published in 1999 by Wayland Publishers Limited

Based on an original text *Kings and Queens – Victoria*
by Richard Wood published in 1995 by Wayland Publishers Limited

First published in 1998 by Wayland Publishers Limited, 61 Western Road, Hove, East Sussex BN3 1JD
© Copyright 1998 Wayland Publishers Limited
Find Wayland on the Internet at http://www.wayland.co.uk

British Library Cataloguing in Publication Data
Stephen, Margaret
Victoria. – (Our kings and queens)
1. Victoria, Queen of Great Britain – Juvenile literature
2. Queens – Great Britain – Biography – Juvenile literature
3. Great Britain – Kings and rulers – Biography – Juvenile literature
4. Great Britain – History – Victoria, 1837–1901 – Juvenile literature
I. Title 941'.081'092
ISBN 0 7502 2583 1

Typeset in England by Raynor Design
Printed and bound by G. Canale & C.S.p.A, Turin, Italy
Cover picture: A portrait of the young Queen Victoria.

All Wayland books encourage children to read and help them improve their literacy.

✓ The contents page, page numbers, headings and index help locate specific pieces of information.

✓ The glossary reinforces alphabetic knowledge and extends vocabulary.

✓ The further information section suggests other books dealing with the same subject.

✓ Find out more about how this book is specifically relevant to the National Literacy Strategy on page 30.

◄ This picture shows Victoria ruling over the law, the Church, the army and the land.

Baby Victoria

In 1819 when Victoria was born, the royal family was not popular. People in Britain did not like King George III, Victoria's grandfather.

Victoria's father, the Duke of Kent, died when she was a baby. The young Victoria was brought up by her German mother. A governess helped to look after her.

Important Dates

1819
Victoria was born.

1837
Victoria became queen.

1897
Queen Victoria's Diamond Jubilee.

▲ The baby Princess Victoria with her parents.

Victoria's childhood

Most people did not think Victoria would ever become queen. But Victoria's grandmother thought that she would. She wrote: 'The English like queens.'

Victoria was not treated like an important princess. She wrote: 'I never had a room to myself till I was nearly grown-up ... We lived in a very simple, plain manner.'

Victoria often played alone with dolls from her large collection.

▲ Victoria drew this picture of her governess.

◄ Princess Victoria with her mother. Victoria loved to dance, sing and play the piano.

▲ Princess Victoria with her dog Dash.

Learning to be queen

As the princess grew older, her mother made sure she would be ready if she became queen. Victoria learnt to speak French, German and Italian. She loved to read books. She also liked to draw the people and places she saw.

When Victoria was eleven years old, she read about kings and queens in history. Then she learned that one day she would be queen. 'I will be good,' she said.

▶ This painting shows Victoria being told that she will be made queen.

When Victoria was thirteen, she travelled around Britain. She saw how ordinary people lived. Her mother gave Victoria a diary so that she could write about her travels. She wrote in her diary every day for the rest of her life.

▲ Victoria saw miners' houses like these on her travels.

In 1837, King William IV, Victoria's uncle, died. Victoria became queen, at the age of eighteen. She wrote in her diary: 'I will do what is fit and right.'

Victoria and Albert

Victoria was crowned at Westminster Abbey. Thousands of people cheered the little queen – she was only 150 cm tall. Many people bought books and plates showing pictures of the coronation.

Most people in Britain were very pleased to have a young queen. But some people thought Victoria was too young.

▲ Victoria is crowned queen.

▶ The young queen meeting her ministers.

People were worried that Victoria would listen to other people and have no ideas of her own. But Victoria was a strong person. She moved into Buckingham Palace, to be away from her mother.

Prince Albert

Victoria had a German cousin called Prince Albert. When he came to England, she fell in love with him. He was good-looking and intelligent. Like Victoria, he enjoyed dancing. It was the happiest moment of her life when he agreed to marry her.

Important Dates

1838
Victoria was crowned queen.

1840
Victoria married Prince Albert.

◄ The wedding of Victoria and Albert. Many brides today wear a white dress like Victoria's.

Family life

Victoria and Albert were married in 1840. Soon they were expecting their first baby. Victoria and Albert did not want servants to bring up their children. So, Albert took charge, and decided how the children should be brought up.

▼ The royal family and their pets in 1843.

Victoria and Albert had nine children. Even when Victoria was pregnant, she carried out all her duties as queen.

Victoria was quite shy. It was hard for her to meet important people from Church and government. She decided to travel away from Buckingham Palace as often as she could.

▲ Christmas trees became popular in Britain after Albert had one at Windsor Castle.

▶ Seven of Victoria's children performing a play in 1854. Victoria was not pleased to see her son Arthur's bare legs.

Royal homes

▲ Osborne House
on the Isle of Wight.

In the 1840s new railways made travelling quicker and easier. The queen could spend more time away from London.

Prince Albert was interested in architecture. He planned Osborne House, a country home on the Isle of Wight. Queen Victoria wrote about it: 'We can walk about anywhere by ourselves without being followed and mobbed.'

Victoria and Albert loved to visit the Highlands of Scotland. They bought an old castle at Balmoral, and had it rebuilt.

The royal family enjoyed walking and climbing in the Highlands. They stayed in small country inns, wearing disguises so that no one would know who they were.

▲ A programme for a play performed at Windsor Castle.

► Queen Victoria with four of her children. The queen is wearing plain Highland clothes.

Life as Queen

Many people thought the queen's life was very exciting. But Victoria worked for many hours every day.

There were always boxes full of government papers for Victoria to read. The queen had to know what was going on all over the world. She spent much of her time signing her name on documents.

Important Dates

1851
Victoria opened the Great Exhibition.

1854–6
The Crimean War.

◄ This cartoon shows Victoria stopping arguments between politicians.

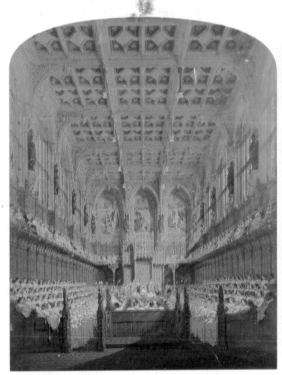

◀ The prime minister had to stand up when he met the queen.

Life was often dull. Every week the prime minister visited the queen to talk about government matters. Some meetings were long. Victoria said: 'I do not think myself that it is good fun to play the queen.'

There were rules for people meeting the queen. People were not allowed to turn their backs on her. They even had to walk out backwards when they left.

▲ Queen Victoria visiting parliament.

The Great Exhibition

Queen Victoria was full of energy. She loved to dance and to go to the theatre. In Scotland she enjoyed walking and climbing in the mountains.

▲ Victoria's dancing shoes.

▼ The Great Exhibition opens.

Victoria also enjoyed some of her official duties. In 1851, she opened the Great Exhibition. Visitors from all over the world went there to see displays of new inventions.

Visiting France

In 1855, Victoria enjoyed a royal visit to France. She and Albert took their two eldest children with them to Paris. Victoria dressed in plain clothes to visit ordinary streets and homes in Paris.

A caring queen

Victoria was a kind person. It upset her to hear of soldiers suffering during the Crimean War. Victoria sent gifts to Florence Nightingale, who nursed the injured soldiers.

▲ A photograph of soldiers at the Crimean War.

Life without Albert

▲ Queen Victoria after Albert died.

Queen Victoria's life changed in 1861, when Prince Albert died. Victoria was heartbroken.

Victoria wrote: 'My life as a happy one is over!' She spent the rest of her long life dressed in black clothes to show how much she missed Albert.

► Victoria visiting her husband's grave.

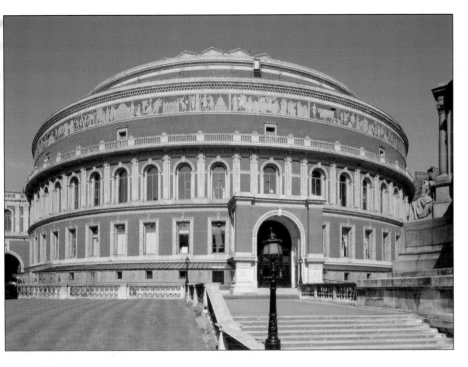

◄ The Royal Albert Hall. It was named after Prince Albert.

The queen soon started to sign papers and meet the prime minister again. But she was so upset after Albert died that she stopped going to public events.

People were not pleased. They wanted to see their queen more often.

Victoria carried out Prince Albert's plans for new buildings in London. She wanted people to remember Albert. The Royal Albert Hall and the Victoria and Albert Museum were named after him.

Important Dates

1861
Albert died.

1871
Victoria opened the Royal Albert Hall.

A lonely time

Victoria continued to show her sadness. When she opened parliament in 1866, she refused to wear her crown or robes.

▲ The wedding of Victoria's eldest son. The queen is in black, watching from the balcony.

Victoria stopped going to the theatre. Actors and singers entertained her at home. The author Charles Dickens was also invited to Buckingham Palace.

Victoria's own writing from her diary was published. She also wrote a popular book about royal life in the Scottish Highlands.

But Victoria missed Albert. After 1863 her closest friend was John Brown. He was her Scottish servant. Some people laughed and called the queen 'Mrs Brown'.

▲ A man trying to kill the queen. She was attacked seven times in her life.

► John Brown holding the queen's horse at Balmoral Castle.

▲ The queen with her servant Munshi. Victoria hated hot rooms. She liked to work outside in this tent.

▼ One of Victoria's prime ministers, William Gladstone.

Servants and ministers

The queen had an Indian servant who taught her to speak his language. He was given the name 'Munshi' which means 'teacher'. Munshi was very bossy, but Victoria listened to his advice.

The queen had to work with many different prime ministers. She disliked some of them, such as William Gladstone.

Benjamin Disraeli was Victoria's favourite prime minister. He tried hard to keep her happy, and tried not to argue with her.

◀ Victoria visiting Disraeli's home.

Fresh air

As Victoria grew older, she spent more time in Scotland. She loved the fresh air there. She did not like stuffy rooms and she hated to see people smoking.

A Popular Queen

Important Dates

1887

Queen Victoria's Golden Jubilee.

► This is an unusual photograph. It shows Victoria smiling.

Many photographs of Queen Victoria when she was old show her looking sad and frowning. But people who knew her did not think she was always sad. They often saw her laughing and smiling.

Victoria was given the title Empress of India. India was one of many countries in the British Empire. Victoria was interested in these countries. She often ate Indian curry. She decorated rooms at Osborne House like Indian rooms.

People celebrated Queen Victoria's Golden Jubilee in 1887. Kings, queens, princes and princesses came from all over the world to see her. She was very popular with the British people again.

▲ This cartoon shows Victoria becoming Empress of India.

► Queen Victoria with royal relatives from Britain, Russia and Germany.

Death of Victoria

After 1890 the queen was not in good health. She still went to Osborne House, Balmoral Castle and France. But she could not take long walks.

Victoria hated to look weak. Even when it rained she went driving in her open carriage.

► Victoria with her son, grandson and great-grandson. They all became kings.

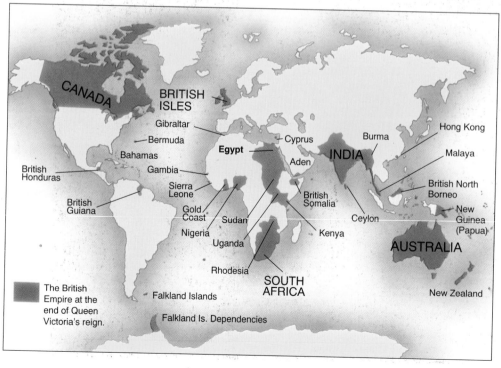

◄ A map showing the countries of the British Empire. They are coloured red.

Many new inventions were made during Victoria's reign. She had flushing lavatories in all her homes. But she did not like telephones. She tried cycling, but she hated motor cars. She was even filmed in moving pictures.

At the end of Victoria's long reign, many people had more comfortable lives than ever before. The British people loved their queen. They felt she had made their lives happier. Queen Victoria died in 1901.

▲ This cup and saucer were made to celebrate the Diamond Jubilee in 1897.

► A photograph of Queen Victoria, taken for her Diamond Jubilee.

Glossary

architecture The art of designing buildings.

cartoon A funny drawing, often about something in the news.

Crimean War The war fought against Russia between 1854 and 1856.

Diamond Jubilee A celebration of Victoria being queen for sixty years.

Empire A large number of countries ruled by one person.

Empress The female ruler of an empire.

Golden Jubilee A celebration of Victoria being queen for fifty years.

governess A woman who is paid to teach children in their own home.

ministers People who help the queen with her work.

parliament The group of politicians who govern Britain.

politicians People who help to run the country.

prime minister The chief minister of the government.

Literacy Information

Children can use this book to improve their literacy skills in the following ways:

- ✓ They can identify the lists of dates in the panels, then locate the same information in the main text.
- ✓ They can use the many headings to locate key pieces of information about the life of Victoria.
- ✓ They can identify what they already know about Victoria, then verify and extend this knowledge using the book.
- ✓ They can look at the quotes in the book and compare this form of writing to the rest of the text.

Books to Read

Famous People, Famous Lives – Queen Victoria by Harriet Castor (Franklin Watts, 1997)

Life and Times – Victoria by John Malam (Wayland, 1998)

Queen Victoria by D. Shearman (Harrap, 1989)

Places to Visit

Buckingham Palace, The Mall, London
Victoria made this her London home.

Holyrood House, Edinburgh
A royal house containing some of Victoria's belongings.

Osborne House, West Cowes, Isle of Wight
This was Victoria's favourite holiday home.

Victoria and Albert Museum, Cromwell Road, London
This museum was opened in memory of Prince Albert.

Picture acknowledgements
The publishers would like to thank the following for permission to publish their pictures: Archie Miles 20 (top); The British Museum 16; Fine Art Photographic Library Ltd 6, 17 (top); Forbes Magazine Collection, London / Bridgeman Art Library, London 10 (top); Guildhall Art Gallery, Corporation of London / Bridgeman Art Library, London 4 (bottom); House of Lords, Westminster, London / Bridgeman Art Library, London 17 (bottom); Getty Images *frontispiece*, 4(top), 14, 18 (bottom), 19, 23 (bottom), 24 (bottom), 25, 26, 27 (both), 28 (top); The Illustrated London News Picture Library 13 (top), 23 (top); The Mansell Collection 9; National Portrait Gallery, London *cover*; Norfolk Museums Service 5, 18 (top), 29 (top); The Royal Archives © 1994 Her Majesty The Queen 13 (bottom), 15 (both), 24 (top); The Royal Collection © 1994 Her Majesty The Queen 7 (both), 8 (both), 10 (bottom), 11, 12, 20 (bottom), 22; Zefa 21. The map on page 28 was supplied by Peter Bull.

Index

Numbers in **bold** refer to pictures and captions.